# Andrew Jackson

## *FRONTIER PATRIOT*

# Andrew Jackson

## *FRONTIER PATRIOT*

*by Louis Sabin*
*illustrated by Dick Smolinski*

**Troll Associates**

*Library of Congress Cataloging in Publication Data*

Sabin, Louis.
    Andrew Jackson, frontier patriot.

    Summary: A biography of the first frontiersman to
become a President of the United States.
    1. Jackson, Andrew, 1767-1845—Juvenile literature.
2. Presidents—United States—Biography—Juvenile
literature.  [1. Jackson, Andrew, 1767-1845.
2. Presidents]  I. Smolinski, Dick, ill.  II. Title.
E382.S23    1986    973.5'6'0924 [B] [92]    85-1094
ISBN 0-8167-0547-X (lib. bdg.)
ISBN 0-8167-0548-8 (pbk.)

# Andrew Jackson

## FRONTIER PATRIOT

Andrew Jackson, the seventh President of the United States, came from a simple, poor background. But his courage, intelligence, and devotion to America brought him greatness and his nation's love. "Old Hickory"—as Jackson was admiringly called for "being as tough as hickory wood"—was a plain-speaking, down-to-earth President. A soldier and a statesman, he made Americans everywhere feel he was one of them.

Andrew Jackson was born on March 15, 1767,
in the Colony of South Carolina. At the time of

his birth, the Jackson family had been in America for just two years. They emigrated from Ireland, where Mr. Jackson was a farmer. Andrew and Elizabeth Hutchinson Jackson, with their two little sons, Hugh and Robert, lived comfortably in Ireland. They were neither rich nor poor. Still, the promise of America appealed strongly to them.

The Jacksons had heard exciting stories about the New World from Mr. Jackson's brother, Hugh. Hugh Jackson had been a soldier in a British regiment sent to fight the American Indians in 1759. It was during the French and Indian War. Hugh spoke of rich lands that were easy to farm—of vast forests, sparkling lakes, and rivers.

They listened, too, to Andrew's brother, Sam. Sam Jackson was a sailor who had visited most of the thriving ports in the Colonies. He described the many busy industries he saw there. Andrew and Elizabeth Jackson were drawn to this exciting new land.

For Mrs. Jackson there were more reasons for traveling to America. Four of her sisters were already living in the New World. Every letter they sent told of opportunities. The four sisters—Jane, Margaret, Mary, and Sarah—all lived within a few miles of each other, in the Colony of South Carolina. Each was married, had a family, and lived on a farm. In their letters to Elizabeth, they described the "Garden of the Waxhaws." Waxhaw was the name of the area where the sisters lived. They said it was a marvelous place to live and prosper.

The letters also said land was cheap, and plenty of it was available. Most of it was good farming land, too. They went on to write that the Indians were no longer a danger to the settlers, that the area was safe and civilized. Best of all, they said, the Jacksons wouldn't have to buy land or build a house right away. They could stay with one of Elizabeth's sisters while they looked around for property.

With great confidence in the future, the Jacksons set sail from Ireland in 1765. After crossing the Atlantic Ocean, their ship landed at Philadelphia, Pennsylvania. There, they bought a horse and wagon and headed south for the Carolinas. The trip took two weeks of steady, difficult travel. They stopped only to cook a meal by the side of the post road or to spend the night sleeping under their wagon. Post roads were major roads which stage-coaches and mail carriers used to travel between cities.

The Hutchinson sisters and their families were delighted when the Jacksons arrived in Waxhaw. It was also a moment of happiness for Elizabeth Jackson. She hadn't seen her sisters for a number of years. Now they were all close again, ready to help each other in every way they could.

Jane Hutchinson Crawford and her husband, James, invited the Jacksons to stay with them. The Crawfords owned a two-story home on a little hill right next to the post road. Downstairs, there was a parlor, a bedroom for Mr. and Mrs. Crawford, and a spacious kitchen where the family ate their meals. Upstairs, there were bedrooms for the children. By pioneer standards, the house was impressive. In fact, it was the largest home in Waxhaw.

After a few weeks with the Crawfords, the Jacksons found a piece of land. It wasn't the most fertile farmland in the area, and it was miles from the nearest road. Even so, the Jacksons bought it because it was the closest available property to Elizabeth's sisters. Helped by their in-laws, the Jacksons worked quickly to build a rough cabin. They also cleared some land and planted a late crop of vegetables and corn. It wasn't a grand start, they admitted, but things would improve with time.

For the next year and a half, Elizabeth and Andrew Jackson worked constantly. However, the poor land did not reward their efforts. Then, in the winter of 1767, the Jacksons faced another concern. Mrs. Jackson was expecting a baby very soon. Her sisters intended to help her when she gave birth. But heavy snowfalls closed the roads and cut off the Jacksons from their relatives.

To make sure Mrs. Jackson stayed warm, Mr. Jackson went out one morning to chop firewood. He wanted to have plenty of logs stacked for the weeks ahead. But as he was lifting a heavy log onto the growing woodpile, Mr. Jackson felt a sharp pain in his chest. He tried to ignore it, but it grew worse, and he staggered into the cabin. He lay down to rest, but that didn't help. Although there is no medical proof, Mr. Jackson probably suffered a severe heart attack. He was dead the next morning.

That same day, a neighbor stopped at the Jackson's place. When he saw what had happened, he swiftly gathered a few of the neighbors. They loaded some of Mrs. Jackson's belongings onto a wagon, put Mrs. Jackson and her children aboard, and took them to the Crawford house. The wagon was followed by a horse-drawn sled carrying Mr. Jackson's coffin.

Mr. Jackson died on March 9, 1767. Just six days later, before sunrise of March 15, Elizabeth Jackson gave birth. It was a boy, and she named him Andrew in honor of her late husband. Andy was a healthy, plump, red-haired infant. He was active from his first day, and his coos and cries filled the house. Even in a home with ten other children demanding attention, Andy made his presence known.

Soon it was spring, which meant planting time for farmers. Mrs. Jackson wanted to take her three children back to their own farm. But she realized she couldn't do that. There was no way for her to plow the field, chop the wood, tend the animals, do all the other chores, and also take proper care of her boys. Besides, her sister, Jane, really needed help.

Jane Crawford was never healthy, and she found it more and more difficult to manage a home and eight children. So she asked Mrs. Jackson to stay. The Crawfords would feed and house the Jacksons. In return, Elizabeth Jackson would take charge of the Crawford household. It was a good arrangement for everyone, and Mrs. Jackson agreed to it.

The Crawford house, in which little Andrew spent his early childhood, was always alive with activity and sound. The children ranged in age from baby Andy to the eldest of the Crawfords, who was a teen-ager. As in any large family, there were plenty of disagreements among the youngsters. The adults tried to keep out of the children's affairs. The house rule was, "Settle it yourself and don't hold a grudge."

For a while, Andrew enjoyed a baby's special treatment. But soon the other children grew tired of giving in to his demands. From then on, Andrew had to stick up for himself or miss out on his share of good things. As the youngest and smallest, he was at a disadvantage. But he soon found a way of overcoming it—with his fists. By the time he began school, at the age of five, Andrew had a reputation as a tough little fighter.

Andy wasn't a mean child. He just did not like being pushed around. He wanted to be like all the other kids, to play the same games, to have the same things. One of the things he wanted most was a Barlow jackknife. It had a small iron blade that folded into a smooth wooden handle. To a child in Colonial days, the Barlow knife was a precious possession. Youngsters saved their pennies for months to buy a Barlow. Once they bought one, they cared for it lovingly. They oiled and polished the wood, and kept the iron blade sharp and free of rust.

Of course, any knife would have done the same job, but the Barlow was considered the best whittling knife made. Throughout the Colonies, whittling, or carving wood, was a favorite pastime for both boys and girls. It was also a skill encouraged by adults. A child might whittle a toy. As an adult, this skill would be used for making furniture, tools, weapons, and household implements. There was an endless supply of wood in the Colonies. So there was no

expense involved beyond the cost of the knife.

Andrew begged and begged for his own Barlow. "No," he was told, "you're too young for a knife of your own." He would have to wait until he reached his seventh birthday. That seemed centuries away to the youngster. So five-year-old Andrew had to settle for the next-best thing. His nine-year-old brother, Hugh, whittled him a bow and some arrows. It was an ideal gift. Andrew spent hours every day, practicing with his bow and arrows.

On Andy's sixth birthday, he received a pop-gun as a present. It, too, was whittled out of a piece of wood. The popgun was the next-best thing to the real rifles the older boys used. Andy enjoyed pretending that he was hunting deer and squirrels with his popgun. Sometimes the older boys even let Andrew shoot a real rifle.

Ordinarily, fathers taught their sons to use a rifle. But since Andrew's father was dead, his older cousins had to teach Andy and his brothers frontier skills. That meant learning to track deer and other wild animals, how to shoot straight, how to take care of their weapons, and how to skin and clean the game they shot. Everyone who lived in the backwoods needed these skills for survival.

Not all of Andrew's days were spent outdoors.
When he was five years old, his mother enrolled
him in the small academy at Waxhaw Church.
The school was run by Dr. William Humphries.

There was another school in the area, which Hugh and Robert attended, but it wasn't as good. At the school Andrew attended, the children learned more than basic reading, writing, and arithmetic. They also studied Latin, Greek, and literature. Among the books they read were John Bunyan's *Pilgrim's Progress, Aesop's Fables,* and Daniel Defoe's *Robinson Crusoe.* Only the brightest of the local children went to this academy.

Andrew was an especially intelligent boy, which is why Mrs. Jackson was willing to spend the extra money for his education. She hoped that Andrew would one day become a minister. He was certainly smart enough to be a minister. Unfortunately, he had a fast temper. He did not hesitate to use his fists when anyone disagreed with him. Although the neighbors wouldn't tell his mother, they all felt that Andrew needed more guidance and a firmer hand.

Elizabeth Jackson did her best, but she was responsible for a household full of children. She couldn't be both father and mother to her sons. Andrew, most of all, suffered from the lack of a father. Hugh and Robert had some memory of Mr. Jackson. Andrew had never known his father.

Young Andrew also felt that the Crawford house was not really his home. He was more like a poor relation, and that feeling bothered him. Although nobody treated him badly, the Jackson boy was aware that he lived in the Crawford house, slept in a Crawford bed, and ate at the Crawford table.

Andrew was too young to understand his feelings. All he knew was that he hated being teased or ignored or picked on by older children. He was small and thin, but he was ready to challenge anyone who tormented him, no matter how big or strong that person was.

The sandy-haired youngster also had a strong code of honor. He never fought with anyone smaller than himself. In fact, he was the protector of the little children. Anyone who picked on a small child did so knowing that Andy might find out. That meant fighting or wrestling with tough little Andy Jackson.

Being so little and thin, Andy was easily knocked down or thrown to the ground. But that didn't end the fight. "I could throw him three times out of four," one of Andrew's schoolmates remembered, "but he would never stay throwed."

Andrew Jackson's boundless energy, stubborn refusal to give up, and his readiness to defend others were important qualities in his adult life. As a general leading troops into battle, he showed great courage and determination, which is why his troops nicknamed him "Old Hickory." Later, as the President of the United States, he was known for his fairness and code of honor. In the oath of office, he swore to protect and defend the Constitution, and all the people of the nation. He took that oath seriously.

Young Andy may have been a fighter, but he wasn't a bully or someone who started arguments for no good reason. As one close friend recalled, "Frolic...not fight, was the ruling interest of Jackson's childhood." He pointed out that Andy was full of spirit. He loved running, swimming, wrestling, and other active sports.

Andrew Jackson was eight years old when the American Revolution began in 1775. His family, like most of the Waxhaw citizens, was eager for news of the battles between the Colonists and the British. All the fighting was going on in the North, and it took a long time for newspapers to reach the South. Newspapers were sent by mail, from Philadelphia, and were carried by a series of riders on horseback. Sometimes weeks passed before the settlers in the Waxhaw got word of events taking place in the North.

It was the middle of August 1776, when a packet of newspapers and a copy of an especially important document reached Waxhaw. Word spread swiftly, and people hurried to the Crawford house to hear the news. Most of the settlers could not read, and they depended on a public reader to tell them what the newspapers had to say.

34

Although Andy was just a schoolboy, he read better than just about anybody else around. For that reason, he was picked to be the public reader as often as any adult.

Andy stood on a chair, surrounded by more than forty people. First, he read aloud accounts of the convention in Philadelphia. Then he read reports of the fighting in New England, of General Washington's troops, and of English ships bringing fresh soldiers to put down the rebellion.

When the newspaper was finished, Andy held up his hand to keep the people from leaving. Then he began to read, *"In Congress, July 4, 1776. The Unanimous Declaration of the Thirteen United States of America. When in the course of human events, it becomes necessary..."* This reading of the Declaration of Independence was the first word that the Waxhaw settlers had that they were citizens of a new nation. They crowded close to young

Andrew, asking him to reread portions of the Declaration. It was an important moment for everyone there, and the memory of it was permanently fixed in Andrew Jackson's mind.

For a while, all the Revolutionary War battles were fought in the North. The only action in the Carolinas was the training of companies of militia. One of these companies was led by Andy's uncle, Captain James Crawford. Andy, who was ten years old, wanted to join up. But he was much too young.

The next year, Andy was invited by the Crawfords to go along on a cattle drive. In those days, cattle ranching was an important business in parts of the South as it would become in the West during the next century. The cattle Andy helped drive to market in Charles Town, South Carolina (today called Charleston), belonged to the Crawfords, to Mrs. Jackson, and to other members of the family. With a war on, beef was needed, and Andy's family hoped to get a good price for it.

The cattle sale was a big success. Mrs. Jackson's share allowed her to send Andrew to a classical boarding school. Here, Andrew could continue his education in Latin and Greek, in addition to religion, botany, penmanship, and basic reading, writing, and mathematics. Unfortunately, Andy did not pay much attention to his studies. He was as bright as ever, but the war was going on, and that meant more to him than school books.

In 1779, when Andy was twelve, his brothers, Hugh and Robert, joined Captain Crawford's company. Andy wanted to go, too, but his mother made him stay in school.

The war reached the Carolinas in the spring of 1780. The British captured Charles Town, and moved inland. Andy's school was closed and all the students were sent home. When he got to his house, Andy learned that Hugh had died after the battle of Stono Ferry. Robert had survived the attack, and was home. The boys helped Mrs. Jackson and the Crawford family pack all their belongings. The British were coming closer, burning houses and taking the horses and cattle. As patriots, the Jacksons and Crawfords were in danger. They had to leave before the British arrived.

Andy and Robert brought their mother and cousins to safety in North Carolina. Then Robert got ready to rejoin Major Crawford's company. This time, Mrs. Jackson could not stop Andy from going along. In July 1780, thirteen-year-old Andrew Jackson enlisted.

Before the war ended, Andy took part in
several battles and was captured by the British.
While he was a prisoner of war, Andy was
ordered to clean the boots of a British officer.
He refused. The angry officer slashed at him
with a sword, cutting the boy's hand and head.
The scar on Andy's head remained visible all his
life, and he was proud of how he had earned it.

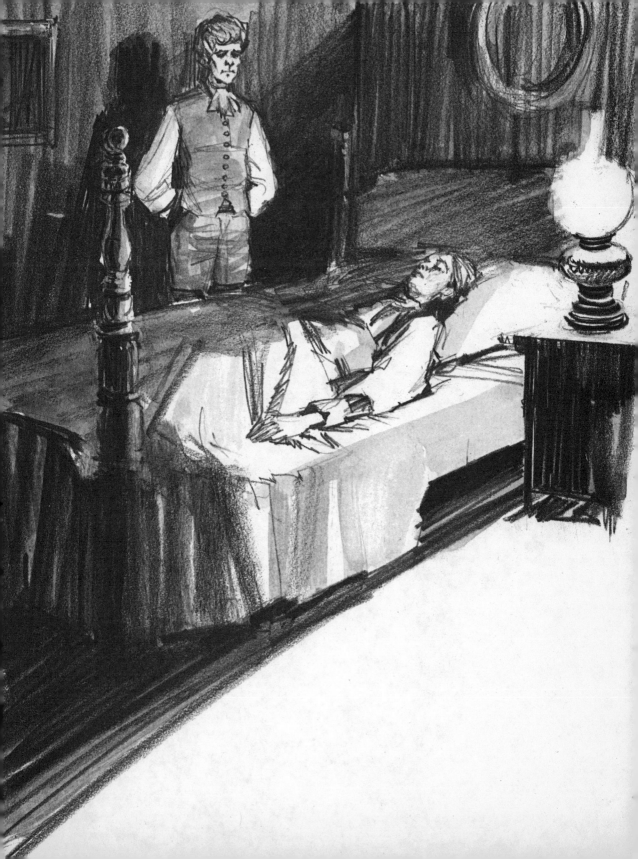

When the war ended, Andrew Jackson was sixteen years old. He was on his own now. In April 1781, his brother Robert had been wounded in battle. The effects of that wound and a smallpox infection soon led to Robert's death. Elizabeth Jackson, Andrew's mother, died of cholera in November of the same year.

"I felt utterly alone," he said later, "and tried to recall her last words to me." Elizabeth Jackson's last words were, "Never tell a lie, nor take what is not your own, nor sue for slander.... Make friends by being honest, keep them by being steadfast."

Andrew Jackson did his best to follow his mother's advice, and to be a sensible young man. But he still had some growing up to do. After Andy inherited a sizable amount of money from one of his grandfathers, he wasted it quickly. This left him almost penniless, but a great deal wiser. Even though he continued to enjoy life, he was never again so foolish with his money.

For a while, Andrew Jackson taught school in Waxhaw. Then, in December 1784, he went to Salisbury, North Carolina to study law. For the next three-and-a-half years, he worked as a law clerk. In that time, the young man read law books and learned to prepare legal documents. That was the way a person became a lawyer in those days. Then, when he was twenty years old, Andrew Jackson became a full-fledged lawyer.

The next year Jackson moved westward, to the town of Nashville, in the territory of Tennessee. There, he bought land and became involved in politics. He was among the leaders in the movement to gain statehood for Tennessee. When Tennessee was admitted to the Union in 1796, Jackson was the new state's first member of the House of Representatives.

In 1797, he left the House of Representatives to serve in the United States Senate. Then he spent ten years as Major-General of the Tennessee Militia. Andrew Jackson now came

to the attention of the United States Army. He was asked to accept a commission as a major-general in the Army. He accepted, and gained widespread fame for his successful defense of New Orleans against the British during the War of 1812.

Jackson became a national hero. After the war, he served as Governor of the territory of Florida, and as United States Senator from Tennessee. In 1828, Andrew Jackson was

elected the seventh President of the United States of America. He served two terms with distinction.

One of the major conflicts during Jackson's administration was the question of nullification. Nullification meant that a state could refuse to obey any federal law it did not like. It could nullify, or cancel, the law. While Jackson was President, South Carolina declared that it would not obey a certain law. Other southern states were threatening to do the same. The issue was a direct challenge to the nation's unity.

President Jackson was a Southerner. He loved the rolling hills of the Carolinas and Tennessee, and he still thought of himself as a son of the South. But he had fought to create the United States, and had seen two brothers die in that fight. Now he was going to defend the United States in a different way—against an internal division. "Our Federal Union—it must be preserved," Jackson declared. He won this fight, too.

In 1837, Andrew Jackson returned to Tennessee, where he died eight years later, on June 8, 1845. He was the first frontiersman to become President, and the first President born west of the Appalachian Mountains. Jackson was the symbol of a growing, expanding America, and of democracy. The nation's political leaders did not believe he would make a good President. But the people had faith in "Old Hickory," and he did not let them down.